Soaring

Jacqueline James

PUBLISHED *by* PARABLES
Earthly Stories with a Heavenly Meaning

Soaring

Jacqueline James

PUBLISHED *by* PARABLES

Earthly Stories with a Heavenly Meaning

Table of Content.

General

Spiritual

Educational

Informative

Entertainment

About the Author

Jacqueline James is a phenomenal poetess with a very unique style of writing. Jacqueline intentions are to bring clarity to her readers (you) through a spiritual perspective, educational awareness and general informative views. She also allows her readers (you) to share her distinctive sense of humor when exploring the entertainment section of her poetry. Jacqueline is a published author who specializes in poetry with a great passion for children stories. She spends countless hours researching different subjects to give (you) her readers the most pleasurable experiences possible when indulging in her work.

The Dedication

This book Soaring is dedicated to (you) the readers for your continuous support.

Sense you have made it this far with me through my amazing writing journey the dedication belongs to (you).

You continue to trust me to inform, educate, uplift, inspire as well as entertain you through my poetry. For these reasons I'm truly grateful and would like to thank you for choosing my work as part of your reading material as a guide to follow.

Introduction

This book Soaring will exhilarate joy and peace through the essence of poetry.

Its contents is intended to soothe the readers (you) into a peaceful euphoria of acceptance for diversity and change.

Each chapter is uniquely categorized to emphasize the importance of its subjects through the reading. The author Jacqueline James carefully selected poems from both personal and educational experiences from her authentic collection to be published in this book. Jacqueline aspirations are for (you) the reader to gain a sense of peace and comfort through the words that God has blessed her to write.

Chapter 1

General

Don't take no wooden nickels...

Everyone has some type of 'hustle',
Rather they're using their brains or using their muscles,
Some fix hair others fix cars,
Some have gardens selling fruit from jars,
Some collect cans and strap metal from the neighborhood,
And others sell discarded items that might be good,
They take them to the recycling plant,
And they sell it for pennies on the pound on a stack,
Now you got the 'bomb-pop' truck driving up and down,
Selling ice cream and frozen treats all around,
During the afternoon hours there's a food truck,
Selling drinks snacks and hot sandwiches for a few bucks,
You got your hand car washers on every other block,
Holding up signs trying to get you to stop,
There are several car lots in between,
Selling new and used cars behind the scenes,
Not to mention the fast food restaurants,
You'll find more than 20 within the radius of five miles,
You can always find a cell phone store,
And if they don't have the phones you looking
for they'll order more,
There's grocery stores convenience stores and dollar stores,
All within walking distance you can buy what you need for sure,
There's liquor stores on every corner,
To make sure you fully intoxicated before the morning,

Now let's not forget the churches up and down the block,
Always honoring each other for extra buck,
There's people selling barbecue and there's a shoeshine man,
And please don't leave out the 'little kids' with the lemonade stand,
There's people standing out raising money for the Girl Scouts,
But don't forget the homeless begging all about,
Everybody has a job to do,
But all the hustlers want something from you,
So don't take no wooden nickels when they're through

He's going to 'pop'...

That boy so greedy he's about to pop,
He needs to exercise ride a bike and walk around the block,
He just sit around the house and eat all day long,
Then he hide food when everybody else is gone,
This boy just refuses to quit,
The more he eats the bigger he gets,
He's always sick and constipated,
When I asked him to relieve himself he hesitated,
At dinner he eats three servings when he sits down,
Then he eats some more when no one else's around,
He doesn't take his health too serious,
But this behavior is starting to worry us,
He loses his manners all the time,
From the toxics that builds up inside,
And if you comment on his behavior,
He'll get defensive and tell the neighbor,
He had to buy new clothes three sizes large,
And he still thinks that he's in charge,
It's not his size I'm worried about,
It's his health and that's no doubt,
He needs to go on a diet and stop eating a lot,
Because if you don't stop 'he's going to pop'!

Out at the 'bar'...

When I'm out,
I 'nurse' the same drink all night,
Enjoying the people the music and the disco lights,
I sit there for hours taking small slips,
I buy the cheapest drink at the club and a waitress expect a tip,
I usually sit around people that I know,
So they'll offer to buy me a second drink before it's time to go,
But it really doesn't matter if they do or if they don't,
Because I didn't come out for the drinks
I came out for the 'small-talk',
You'll be surprised on how much people have to say,
When they stopped in a 'bar' for a drink at the end of their day,
You'll meet all types of people from every walks of life,
Who just stopped by to release a 'little' steam
before the end of the night,
Everyone who comes in has a different story to tell,
About their life situation rather it's just fine or not so well,
Some of the people who come in don't want to be bother,
They like to sit to themselves drink and drown
their 'sorrows' in a bottle,
One thing we all have in common,
is that we like the music playing loud,
And none of us mind the drunken crowd,
Sometimes I've gotten so 'full' I needed an escort to my car,
Those were unforgettable times out at the 'bar'.

Getting 'Older'...

I thought I was a bowl of cereal much as my bones 'popped',
And when I walk my knees 'knock',
I've gotten older and I'm about 'falling' apart,
But lucky for me I have a strong heart,
However the rest I think is glued together,
Because I start hurting and aching all over with the
change of the weather,
I take aspirin cause my head hurts all the time,
But when I nap all day I feel just fine,
My neck 'pops' when I turn my head from side-to-side,
And I keep a 'crook' in it that I try to hide,
My arms hurt when I stretch them out wide,
And when I move around I feel cramps in my side,
All of my joints 'pop' as I move about,
And I wonder what that's-about?
But I don't open my mouth,
My back hurts rather I'm walking standing or sitting down,
And if I stand too long I lose my balance and fall,
I got arthritis in my fingers and my hands,
And my legs are so weak I can barely stand,
My feet swells up as I move about,
And the back of my legs hurt cause I have 'gout',
All my toenails are all overgrown,
I tried to clip them myself but I couldn't reach them on my own,
I pass gas all day long,

And I look around and see what's smelling so 'foul,"
I'm trying to talk on the phone but I can't hardly hear,
I'm wondering if there's something wrong with my ear?
I constantly repeat myself,
I'll convinced myself it happened as I waste my breath,
I'm stressing when I drive a car,
And it doesn't matter if I'm not going far,
It feels like the weight of the world is on my shoulders,
And if I didn't know better I'll say "I was getting older",
And as-for-as my mind it's sharp as-can-be,
If I could just remember who was talking to me!

From the Middle...

From the bottom to the top,
From the top to the bottom,
If you want the middle all you have to do is 'holla',
From the end to the out,
From the out to the end,
If you want the middle all you have to do is 'bend',
From the off to the on,
From the on to the off,
If you want the middle then you have to close your 'mouth',
From the down to the up,
From the up to the down,
If you want the middle then you have to come around,
From the under to the over,
From the over to the under,
If you want to middle then you have to feel the thunder,
From the close to the open,
From the open to the close,
If you want the middle then it's whatever goes,
From the back to the front,
From the front to the back,
If you want the middle there'll be no slack,
From the old to the young,
From the young to the old,
If you want the middle then be real bold,
From the cold to the hot,

From the hot to the cold,
If you want the middle it's put on hold,
From the new to the used,
From the used to the new,
If you want the middle then I do too!

Plus Size Women...

If you're a plus size woman don't lose your self-esteem,
Being 'petite' isn't for every woman it may be a bad dream,
Dress your best to be your best,
Take care of yourself and don't settle for less,
Plus size women you're looking good with all of your curve,
Whoever don't agree then they got their nerves,
It's really nice to be a 'few' sizes bigger,
Because you're 'shade' in the summer time,
And you're 'warmth' in the winter,
Embrace yourself and all that you do,
Cause those 'skinny-chic's' are trying to eat more to look like you,
They wish they had your big round 'hip',
With your thick-thighs and you can still do a 'split',
They had no idea that you were that flexible,
Because they're stiff as a 'broad' and they didn't think
it was possible,
Yeah you're large however you're in good shape,
You're big in the 'waste' but you're 'cute' in the 'face'!
So watch-out 'skinny-girls' cause 'thick' is in,
Go gain a 'few' extra pounds if you want to be our friend.

Mississippi Cruise...

I'm out and down went the sun,
Now I'm on riverboat having fun,
It's my birthday weekend,
And I came out with a friend,
We just wanted to 'turn-up' for the night,
Cruising the Mississippi by moon light,
The boat was full with lots of souls,
We were all singing and dancing out of control,
The captain when over some safety rules,
Then the boat started to move when he was through,
The 'DJ' played all the latest songs,
I danced all night but I wasn't alone,
He played all the right songs,
That kept everyone on the dance floor all night long,
We sailed the river by the night tide,
With nothing but 'partly-people' on the boat ride,
We celebrated birthdays as we float,
And we stump and jumped until we rocked the boat,
We had all the fun that 'one' could possibly have,
All this laughter on my behalf,
We rocked the boat while it was out,
With less than twenty minutes before we docked,
We all came back with no regrets,
Just filled with good memories we'll never forget.

The Attraction...

I met a man a stranger to my eyes,
He was 'into' me to my surprise,
I was flirting just having some fun,
But we had chemistry was he the one?
I was on vacation with three girlfriends,
I was acting 'fast' just trying to fit in,
It was actually a 'dare' that I willing except,
To flirt with a stranger just for laughs,
As it turned out he was a man of statute,
He was filled with integrity and blushed when I approached him,
At that moment I tried to dismiss the thought,
However the attraction was there and we both were caught,
He held my hand intentionally taking the lead,
His masculinity capture a spark in me indeed,
I had my entire trip planned with the 'girl's',
But unconsciously I was plotting on how
I could fit him into my world,
The city that I visiting was his home town,
I live five hours away and had no idea when I'd be back around,
We shared an intense conversation,
It was filled with passion with a romantic connection,
He gave a gentle kiss as he walked me to the door,
With the reassurance that he wanted to see me some more.

Go Through...

We must go through something,
In-order-to get to something,
Humiliation builds humility,
Great character brings agility,
Perseverance brings completion,
Determination is for that reason,
Motivation produces adrenaline,
And your loyalty makes you genuine,
There's always something each day that's new,
And these are the things that we must go through.

The Rally...

I was invited to come out for a 'rally',
With enough food and drinks for everybody,
We came out to speak of the brutality in the LGBT community,
As we spoke of the cruelty it brought us closer together in unity
All the people I met were on point,
I felt all good vibes from the start,
Their difference were quite alright,
They were true to themselves and that-I liked,
There was so much raw talent in the room,
I could picture them mastering their 'crafts' very soon,
It was impossible to measure all the love that was in the air,
I came out to mingle and I was glad to be there,
It was young adults from different walks of life,
Filled with ambition ready for life's fight,
Each one of them held a promising future,
And with their raging spirits it wouldn't remain neutral,
As I sat there listening to each one of them speak,
I felt the strength of warriors rising to the mountains peak,
Their spirits were mellow to my surprise,
We were all on one accord-we harmonized,
We sat in a circle and did a 'sage' cleansing to free ourselves,
And when we were done venting there wasn't any negativity left,
It was my first time experiencing something so liberal and free,
Afterwards I knew it was the right place to be,
I felt a weight lifted from my shoulders,

And the atmosphere was covered with love and peace from my
sisters and brothers,
Each one of us took turns stating what we loved about ourselves,
When it was my turn I read a poem that spoke for itself
Then it turned out to be a 'ripple-effect',
It was other poets among us that were just as blessed,
So we all begin to share our unique given style,
Then the laughter and fun 'blasted' on for a while,
Some played their favorite songs when they got a chance,
Because they just preferred to get up and dance,
I met a lot of new friends all different kinds,
And it doesn't really matter because now they're all mine,
Nevertheless we made memories that will be ours forever,
Which I'll hold 'dear' in my heart until new ones develop!

My twisted ankle...

I twist my ankle and it was swollen as could be,
I wouldn't wish this on my worst enemy,
My mama came over with some home remedies,
She soak my ankle, rubbed my ankle, then put an ice pack on it
which was very cold to me,
She brought me some food to eat but I didn't want none,
I just laid in the bed with my ankle cold and numb,
I imagined myself going to use the restroom hopping on one leg,
Then she said "girl you better lay yourself still don't you
get out of that bed"
I was going to use that restroom if I had to crawl all the way to it,
Because using a 'bedpan' I will refuse to do it,
Now my ankle had started to swell and it was hurting,
My daughter gave me two pain patches which finally start working,
So I hobbled on to the restroom and relieve myself,
I took two pain pills afterwards but I don't know how I felt,
Sleep or just lying there-either way,
I was in my bed for the rest of the day,
I laid there and try to watch the television for a little while,
Even though I knew it wasn't exactly my style,
I started dozing in-and-out of consciousness,
Until eventually sleep got the best of me and I had to rest,
I woke up a few hours later and I must've been confused,
When I step down on my foot my ankle 'pop' and I got bad news,
"Ouch" I was in excruciating pain at this point,

It was more than my ankle the pain radiating through my joints,
Time to go to the doctor first thing I thought,
But I dreaded that visit I even fought,
So I called my mother and told her what happened,
She brought over her 'walking- boot' from when she was limping,
This saved me a trip to the doctor and the hospital bill,
So I wrap my ankle put on the boot and walked around still,
I didn't need a doctor to tell me to stay off of my feet,
I just needed to take it easy for a couple of week,
It took some time for my ankle to get better,
I was truly happy that the pain didn't last forever.

That 'Sound'...

You sound so good you sound like the man I fell in love with,
You sound so wise the strength in your voice I'll never forget,
Your strong yet gentle touch,
Is everything about you that meant so much,
I'm walking backwards through a mist of time,
To fill a void from the love-once was mind,
One step away and two steps backwards,
From the misplaced heart that's bound to trap me,
A moment of weakness from a shattered thought,
My knees are knocking trying to bring me out,
By the 'sound' of your voice I'm mesmerize,
With a tip of your touch before my eyes,
Longing to find our love again,
Darling no! I can't be your friend,
Just let me hold your hand so I can see,
Whatever works for you will work for me,
I know looking back it's just an illusion,
A trail of pain was our conclusion,
Why do you sound so good after it's all over?
Have I made you better for another lover?
I was there I was willing to commit,

But you were no longer the man I fell in love with,
Now I wonder from the sound of your voice,
I have no regrets I made my choice,
I feel your peace when you're around,
I know you're content by the way you sound.

Thoughts in my head

There's thoughts running through my head like bees buzzing,
If I stop talking they'll start to get fuzzy,
If you ask I can't recollect what I just said,
Cause of all these thoughts running through my head,
I speak all the time in a rhyme,
These thoughts are not yours they're mine,
All my thoughts of the day are reformed,
Then they come out in the form of a poem,
I can't possibly stop them if I try,
Their 'will' controls me and I can't deny,
They're in my head but needs to come out,
That's what my poems are all about,
I write them down to release the thought,
And before long some more comes about,
I write and write until I'm tired,
But there's more to come that's still inside,
So I write as much as I possibly can,
I write what they want on demand,
They make me write when I'm up,
And they make write when I lay down,
Once I start writing they don't make a sound,
But if I stop they bring my thoughts back to where I left off,
So good or bad they're thoughts in my head,
They're here to stay that's what I said!

Chapter 2

Spiritual

Revival

Revive me Lord purify my thoughts,
Wash me clean and bring me out,
Cover me with your precious blood,
So, I'll be fill with my 'Father's' love,
Revive me Lord help me to see Your "will" so clear,
Stay with me Lord linger near,
Help me daily through Your grace,
Keep me worthy to see my 'Father's' face,
Save my soul and set me free,
Remove the shackles from my feet,
Revive me Lord keep me raging with your peace,
Help my faith in You increase,
Tame my spirit and my tongue,
Fill my heart with love and joy,
Revive me Lord fill me with Your Holy Ghost,
Separate me from other folks,
Help me learn Your daily bread,
Through Your word is how I'm fed,
Help me with the world's temptation,
Bless me with God's revelation,

Revive me Lord help me see,
All Your blessings in stored for me,
Bless my heart with Your love I'll receive,
Keep me filled with Your word I'll believe,
Bless me 'Father' while I'm alive,
Save my soul so it's revived!

Fallen 'Angels'...

Fallen angels from the sky,
We often wonder why they die,
To move through this world so free,
Making a connection from you through me,
Giving love while they're here,
Moving quickly through the atmosphere,
Wanting more than just your time,
Bringing about a peace of mind,
Helping the living in 'life' form,
Their time is limited when they come,
Sharing with the world lots of joy,
Born through the form of a 'girl' or 'boy',
When their 'time' here is up and they have to go,
We'll try to prolong it because we want them more,
Sometimes we meet them as a peaceful stranger,
However they're really God's fallen 'angels'.

My Inspiration...

I got my inspiration through a spiritual insight,
While lying in the bed writing through the night,
God sends the words straight to my soul,
They're not mine He's in control,
I'm just obedient to God's 'will',
All His blessings He continues to give,
From the heavens I receive my words,
Unlike anything you've ever heard,
My message are meant to inspire,
The more you hear the more you're sure to desire,
He fills me up with things that's great,
And I write them down for 'heaven's' sake,
The more I write the more they come,
And they're all filled up with Jesus love,
How I get my inspiration,
I look around at God's creation,
Of all the things that one can mention,
My writing gets my full attention,
I give my best at any given situation,
I'm fully committed with dedication,
The messages come through a spiritual revelation,
That fills me up with inspiration.

The Church of the Living God...

The church is the only institution that can reach into the pits of
'hell' and pull out a soul,
Through the power of prayer God's in control,
When Gods people come together and pray on one accord,
Deliverance will come when you cry out unto the Lord,
Souls are saved body sore healed,
All sickness is overcome when God's miracles are revealed,
Satan has to cease when God takes over,
Salvation is given and through Jesus blood we're covered,
Just have a 'little' talk with Jesus it'll be alright,
God will deliver you day or night,
There's power in the name of Jesus,
Through your prayer you can call on Him for any reason,
No weapon formed against you shall prosper,
When you have Jesus as your comforter,
All of God's 'saints' worship together in the church,
They pray for deliverance from all destruction and hurt,
They trust in their healing from 'Our Father' above,
And for complete deliverance through His love,
I thank God for his sanctuary,
Because of His ministers I don't have to worry,
The church of the living God is put in place,

To save 'souls' from being displaced,
God has ordained the ministers with the 'Holy Ghost' power,
To save the 'lost' in their final hour.
'.

Death at the door...

Death with the anticipation to die,
When you've been giving a reason why,
None of us knows the actual hour or minute,
So we push our lives to the limit,
But when our diagnosis is terminally ill,
Then death certainly becomes very real,
Some of us immediately start to make a 'bucket list',
With all the things on it from life we thought we missed,
While insisting on getting some fulfillment from their last days,
Other's just wait helplessly and pray,
Although death is inevitable to every living creature,
We try to enhance it by prolonging it through various features,
We take excessive amounts and high doses of medications
We've gone through strenuous treatments and endured its
complications
From drugs prescribed that were powerful and strong,
That kept one sick and weak while trying to prolong,
Nevertheless it's coming death is on its way,
Some of us have gotten 'bitter' needless to say,
Some of us have shut down and didn't want to be bothered,
Others become aggressive because they're cowards,
It's hard to embrace death head-on,
Because you know in the end you're facing it alone,

There's talk of a 'light' after all goes dark,
But how can you know of a journey that you never embarked,
There is comfort to know if your soul is clean,
And you'll rest in peace in heaven after everything,
You'll meet your 'creator' His name is God,
That'll make your death-dying all worthwhile,
So if you're given a death sentence and deaths at your door,
Just keep your faith in Jesus and don't worry no more!

The 'fruit' that bears...

Judge the 'tree' by the fruit it bears,
But not always by the things you hear,
Bear witness to the false prophets around,
For their messages may not be that of God,
We are the 'sheep' the fruit of our labor,
We pray to God to show us favor,
From the 'clergy's' or the leader of the church,
And we accept their words for what it's worth,
But God gave us knowledge to study His 'word' on our own,
That we may know if they're right or wrong,
Some people have used the bible for their convenience,
Which they weren't teaching of God's 'holy' reason,
Every 'clergy' that preach is not anointed,
They weren't chosen they were only appointed,
Therefore their congregations is filled with contempt,
Having malice in their hearts without repent,
So when you look at the 'tree' it is the leader,
Bearing 'fruits' of corruption and breeding 'sinners',

Chapter 3

Educational

1. All the Things...
2 Every=All...
3. Judge the Word...
4. Far from "Harmless"...
5. The Brain Injury...
6. The Beauty Within us...

All the things...

All the things that I wanted to do,
I miss just doing it don't you?
All the things that I wanted to say,
I miss you saying it anyway,
All the things I was supposed to see,
I missed you seeing what was supposed to be,
All the things I was supposed to do,
I miss just doing them don't you too?
All the things I was supposed to have,
I miss just having them just for laughs,
All the places I was supposed to go,
I miss just going just for show,
All the things I was supposed to know,
I miss just knowing that's how it goes,
All the things I was supposed to feel,
I miss just feeling it and that's for real,
All the way I was supposed to act,
I miss just acting and that's a fact,
All the while I was supposed to live,
I miss just living and that's for real,
All the days I was supposed to spend,
I missed just spending them with a friend,
All the reasons I was supposed to cry,
I miss just crying and I wondered why,
All the things I was supposed to learn,

I miss just learning it now it's gone,
All the reasons I was supposed to pout,
I miss pouting now I shout,
All the places I was suppose to go,
I missed going now don't you?
All the reasons I was supposed to write,
I wrote them down and got them right,
All the days I was suppose to pray,
I prayed to God and Jesus stayed!

Every = All...

Every-equals-all,
Who has the right to make 'that' call?
Up against the world I'm different,
I don't get the 'right' to complain who's listening,
Bowing down from the surface of my skin,
Stressing to express my wonders from within,
Unlike you-I'm me having to conform to be free,
Special is why I'm here isolated because of your fear,
I am trapped between the grips of your hold,
Because of my preference I have no control,
My pain raging because I'm not understood,
You'd sympathize only if you could,
Majority wins your thoughts are of the crowd,
And if necessary you'll shout them out loud,
You gets to decide rather you're right or wrong,
That leave me hopeless left out on my own,
Do you think that I chose to be different this way,
To be ridiculed and judged every single day,
I fight for 'me' when you turn your back,
Everyone's the same and that's a proven fact,
I stand for 'all'-'all' the ridicule and nonsense,
I fall for 'every'-'every' thing that's past tense,
Every-equals-all to everything that matters,
Every-equals-all until my life gets better.

Judge the world...

Drawn in through sophistication,
Bringing about more civil communication,
Reluctant to deal with the uneducated,
Or those who's not loyal or dedicated,
Your mind is set on a certain kind,
If you searched diligently then you will find,
Then you'll sit around and judge the world,
As if only you wore diamonds and pearls,
You're in a 'group' with others like you,
That have certain standards to carry through.
You think you're the best of the world's creations,
Everyone has issues from their own situations,
You might be rich sophisticated with 'stats',
Nevertheless you'll have your own trials and tribulations
and that's sure fact,
You refuse to recognize me as being of any importance,
So you alienated me before your subordinates,
While you're judging me for the things I may or may not do,
Remember when you point your finger your thumb is pointing
back at you!

Far from 'Harmless'...

I write about everything I do at the end of each night,
But the things I did today just wasn't quite right,
There's this homeless man that's really bothering me a lot,
He's sleeping in the vacant house next door and he's drinking
alcohol on the property lot,
But that's not what has me in the uproar,
This man is on the sex offender registry and he's hurt
children before,
He turned a bucket upside down and was looking into my
daughter's bathroom window,
When the police came he surrendered, my question is why the
police let him right back out,
He was free the next day to drink and roaming about,
Now he steady camping out next door on the front porch,
So I keep dialing 911 but it's like I'm just wasting my voice,
Every time they show up and run this man away,
He just walks down the street and then comes back the same day,
The police told me that the owner of the house must
file a complaint,
However the owner has moved away and left the house to rented at
a later date,
The police tried to reassure me that this man wasn't
harmful just homeless,
I have sympathy for the homeless but not for a pedophile,
And if he's on the sex offender registry that means he's been

mischief for a while,
This man maybe homeless but he's far from harmless,
I don't want him around spreading his poison,
Shame on the police for not doing what's right,
Keeping this man off my street so I can sleep peacefully at night.

The Brain Injury...

My son got a scholarship today for being hit in the head,
I was just truly blessed that he didn't end up dead,
A television set fell on his head when he was 2 years old,
He was in the hospital for 3 Days having seizures and (why) the
doctors didn't even know,
I was told from his 'daycare' that he just collapsed one day and
start having a seizure,
But he had a brain injury and that was the reason,
All of the workers lied to cover up their actions,
But the 'cook' came forward with the true confession,
I was truly grateful because now the doctors knew
how to treat him,
They no longer had to run test to determine why he was
weak in his limbs,
They discontinue the medicines that he was on,
Because now they knew with certainty where his
seizures were from,
The 'cook' got fired after she came forward,
But I'm forever grateful cause the rest of them were cowards,
This incident change the course of my son life,
He grew up going to occupational therapy speech therapy and
physical therapy and he still continues to fight,
I don't quite remember him being "the average child",
As he grew up I ran him back and forth to different doctors the
entire while,

He spent his entire life on medication and trying to fit in,
And other than his siblings I'm his closest friend,
He graduated from high school and he completed 'College' as well,
It took a 'little' extra time but he came out just swell,
I'm so proud of him on so many levels,
My son is very brave and he's also clever,
Now he going to the university to continue his education,
And I'm confident he'll achieve his goals
because of his dedication,
But I thank God for the struggle that he came through,
Because (today) he was presented with a scholarship, along with
an award and I was able to share 'his' story with you!

The Beauty Within Us...

From songs to sing with great 'harmony',
Filled with the perfect melodies,
Clergies have their sermons to preach with the right words to say,
Helping the 'saints' to have a blessed day,
For 'chefs' to cook a dish so divine,
Serving up recipes that's one of a kind,
The 'seamstress' have their clothes to sew,
With different designs we wear and off we go,
Now the 'banker' has his money to count,
And we trust him with ours to figure it out,
Now there's 'racers' to run a marathon,
And they wants to come in first place to beat the crowd,
How about the 'drivers' who chauffeurs you around,
Who've seen the world and know the town,
Let's not forget the 'doctors with their expertise and knowledge,
Prescribing medicines with healing power,
Now you got 'DJ's' playing the right songs,
Making sure the party goes on all night long,
There are 'teachers' who teaches a valuable lesson,
Educating many through their profession,
You get a 'hair dresser' that creates there spectacular styles,
So that we'll walk around looking glamorous for a while,
There's 'architects' who design the structures on their own,
Making our unique and perfect home,
There's 'writers' who write the precise words,

Bringing encouragement through their messages that's heard,

God has blessed all the 'beauty within us,
Through His grace we live we trust,
And for an 'artist' to pant the beauty in me,
For his talent to show and the world to see,
And now myself the 'poet' filled with rhymes,
Blessed with original talent from inside!

Chapter 4

No More...

It is sickening and it saddens me to know that my beautiful black
people have been under bondage in such a horrific way,
They're still suffering with depression to this very day,
However there's no need for oppression because other nationalities
have been under captivity and slavery as well,
They too have some horrible stories to share that weren't so swell,
We're neither less than nor above but equal to with all rights of
love from our mothers,
And though our 'Father' in heaven we're all sisters and brothers,
We've suffered by the hands of our oppressors,
Our generations has the strength of warriors from our ancestors,
I'm asking you to reach beyond your circumstances
Get a grip on your life and make some demands,
Nothing is easy however it's worth working and fighting for to
make a stand,
With self-respect and self-control we can forced society to raise the
'bar',
Black people we have been bullied by white
supremacist for so long,
Their brutal treatment is profound,
Society is tired of hearing the same old song,
However they're the ones as a whole that continue to do us wrong,
Let's insert our power and let's do it now,
By standing up for ourselves and sticking together we can show
them how,

We are a much divided race of people,
We get malice for my own kind who refuse to greet us,
Unfortunately there is bullying everywhere you go,
It isn't just from the "white people" you know,
Stop living as the victims and become the conquerors,
Master your skills and obtain a doctrine,
Our minds are the only thing that's going to
get us past these predicaments,
We must rise up and stay determined with strong convictions,
We have to stand together strong and say no more
And even be willing to settle the score,
Yes I'm about peace with a peace offering,
However I refuse to stand back and watch all my people
end up in a coffin,
Stand united with me and say no more,
I guarantee you no one wants a civil war

Cousins...

Cousins they're everywhere,
Always showing how much they care,
I went to a 'home going service' and a lot of mine were there,
Mourning and grieving because they care,
Half of us didn't know each other,
But we knew we were cousin to each other,
Either we were cousins on our mother's side,
Or we were related through marriage and just came along
for the ride,
If we are cousins on our father side,
Then our parents should've introduced us and swallow their pride,
In some cases your parents are separated too soon,
Then we never found out who was related to who,
We don't always grow up with each other,
We might've been born out of wedlock from our mother's lover,
Nevertheless we're related cause we're cousins,
If you don't meet your cousin soon enough,
You could possibly end up dating them as of such,
I'm not joking this thing is for real,
I dated my cousin and it made me ill,
Even though we were cousins through marriage
and no blood relations,
When I found out I end it without hesitation,
It was a new family in my church congregation,
I found out we were cousins and we're blood-related,

He's my father's mother-first-cousins-grandson,
He has a wife a daughters and two sons,
That makes him my fourth cousins and his kids my fifth cousins
through the generation,
Either way we're all cousins and we're all related,
Everyone need to know their family history,
Before they end up dating their cousins and possibly kissing.

The Illness...

First she was weak then she started to feel better,
She had gotten so much strength she was walking around yelling,
She must have gotten an adrenaline rush,
Because she became confrontational and started to fuss,
Maybe her illness was only temporary,
Or she took it lightly because she refused to worry,
Nevertheless she was up walking around,
Ready to get into mischief and perhaps clown
I tried to stay clear of her threatening ways,
However she insisted that I stay,
I stayed despite of my better judgement,
Then she got 'worked-up' over a noise that scare her,
The noise startled everyone in the room,
However she reacted with violence and didn't calm down soon,
She started throwing the furniture all around,
A chair went across the floor and a lamp hit the ground,
We looked at each other in a big shock,
All wondering when was she going to stop?
Her outburst continue for a while,
Until the paramedics was called to calm her down,
She was taken to a hospital from the situation,
The doctor suggested she stay overnight for observation,
The next day when she was discharged,
Her family wanted her home but they did look forward,
Nevertheless they picked her up with a promising note,

The doctor had prescribed some medicine to help her cope,
She was diagnosis with having the condition schizophrenia,
That alone may the whole house panic,
They said she was hearing voices and couldn't help herself,
She needed to be watched closely before she hurts someone else,
The family had an important decision ahead of them,
Can they handled this situation or will it be too much,
They loved her dearly but she needed professional help,
They checked her in a facility then they left,
They visit her often as they could,
Eventually they stopped because she didn't know who they were,
Unfortunately there's no cure for the type of illness she had,
This broke our hearts and made us sad,
The medication she was taking had to be increased,
However she lived her final days out in peace.

Mourning 2 Loses...

Mourning two losses,
I lost a friend and an ex-lover at what cost?
My friend was my oldest sister who I often talk too,
Now that she's gone I have no idea what I should do,
My lover was my ex-husband who I had to get over,
Even after our divorce he held a special place in my heart
unlike no other,
My sister meant the world to me,
However her body was sick and everyone could see,
Whenever I'm sad or confused,
I still long for her advice to carry me through,
My sister died and I miss her every day and every night,
I watched her life slip away as she put up a fight,
I admired her resilience and all that she had to offer,
It broke my heart when I saw her lying in her coffin,

My ex and I had been separated for a while,
And he took up with another and fathered a child,
Even though we both moved on in different directions,
His presence stayed strong and I felted his protection,

When I got a call that my ex-husband had gotten killed,
My life started to shatter because I didn't know how to feel,
So I went through the motions of the grieving process,

And I tried to stay strong I even tried my best,
But all of the pain I was filling from the start,
It just over lapped each other and flooded my heart.

My 'Business' Plan...

Opportunity is what you have in your hand,
From my uniquely written business plan,
After you indulge me you will learn,
That my loyalty and trust you have earned,
I wrote it up in a crafty way,
To brighten your thoughts throughout the day,
The first thing was my mission statement,
"To reach the people with something greater",
Then it starts with the financial section,
Equally balanced to perfection,
Explaining all of the potential profits,
And leaving room for future offers,
Then it goes to my true objective,
Making sure your investment's protected,
Then I state my action plan,
How to be inspired on demand,
Now to reach my targeted audience,
Everyone who has a heart in 'them',
Don't forget my marketing skills,
Sharing with the world on how I feel,
I'll write it once and read it twice,
Making sure my words are extra nice,
I plan to reach the world you'll see,
And share a 'little' part of me,
I want my words read in every language,

To motivate friends-to-strangers,
Now I'll show you my yearly projection,
With guarantees of satisfaction,
Now you want by employee list,
You're listening to 'it' I'm the best,
And for my over-all goal,
It's to inspire you all and take control,
Since you've read my 'business-plan',
I've just acquire a brand new 'fan'!

After You...

After you look twice to see your part,
You might just have a change of heart,
After everything is said and done,
You might just realize why you didn't run,
After it gets close to the end,
You might just consider him as a friend,
After you get over all your thoughts,
You might just start to figure things out,
After you get past your doubtful ways,
You might just have some brighter days,
After you start to feel your peace,
You might just find your pain has ceased,
After you forgive the things he's done,
You might just start to have some fun.

I am a poet true and free...

I am a poet true and free,
My poetry is what defines me,
I am powerful I am strong,
When I write poetry I stand alone,
I am gifted I'm also blessed,
When my Lord writes through me it's the very best,
I'm always available I am on call,
To deliver God messages to reach you all,
I am unique my style is great,
I write for hours I stay up late,
I am loving and I am caring,
I'm mostly happy when I'm sharing,
I am courageous and I write the truth,
I write about myself and I'll write about you,
I'll bring about clarity and I give purpose,
The things I write is always worth it,
I am a poet true and free,
My poetry is what defines me.

In Between My 'Happenings'...

Something happened in between my 'happenings',
It rushed around as it was grabbing me,
It snatched the thoughts inside itself,
It made me cry with nothing left,
I laughed about and played beneath,
This dark side was not complete,
I danced around beneath the scene,
My heart shattered as my ears did ring,
My 'happenings' covered my whole day long,
I rose above my own sad song,
Life pick me up and tossed me back down,
It crowd my thoughts when death came around,
I laughed about as I tour the town,
Inside my smile I wore a frown,
I draw a blank my 'stick' was short,
It closed on in and broke my heart,
I felt it's pain it pierced real deep,
I danced some more it made me weak,
It jumped right in to claim my day,
I played as long as it wanted to stay,
I danced about it swallowed me whole,

I laughed some more I took control,
It started up to close my mind,
I prayed to God for peace to find.

The 'Transfer'...

I had never heard of the word 'manipulation',
I wasn't expecting the students to be so cruel through their
association,
I was new to the area and needed a friend,
I had been uprooted from my comfort zone where my
childhood began,
Where I grew up the neighbors could chastise you,
Then your parents would further your discipline when
they were through,
We walked miles to commute back and forth to school each day,
Rain snow sleet or hail we didn't stray,
We were just giving the comfort of indoor recess on a freezing day,
Nevertheless we adapted to our situation and conquered
it our own way,
We were not spoon-fed nor did we expect a handout,
We survived our own reality each day when we went out,
The adults in my neighborhood wasn't raping kidnapping or killing
little children,
They were all expected to be a role model if they could have,
They weren't all perfect they had their own flaws,
Nevertheless we stayed in a 'child's place' and didn't inter-act until
we were allowed,
If you had a good report card or special talent you'll be called in
the room to 'show-off' among the adults,
But if you entered without their permission you'd get your little

'butt' torn-up,
We had respect for our elders and were obedient,
We knew when an adult said something they meant it,
We didn't challenge authority or make a scene,
We were raised with morals and 'Christian' values not
worldly things,
All the children were allowed to stay out until 8 p.m.,
When the streetlights came on they knew to come in,
We play games like jump rope marbles or 'Rock Teacher',
We play hide-and-go-seek we rode our bikes and sometimes we
just sat on our porch to greet you,
Our parents clothed us fed us and provided for us but they weren't
our friends,
They loved us and provided plenty,
I grew up in the heart of the city,
Where things weren't always so pretty,
It was abandoned houses lots of poverty in a slum neighborhood,
Our parents struggles was real and they did the best we could,
It was lots of unemployment however everybody had a different
hustle going,
Some days was filled with drinking gambling and partying it was
never boring,
But everyone was always trying to get ahead of their
present situation,
By vowing to move out and working hard with dedication,
We were some of the 'lucky' ones who fought,
We moved out of the 'ghetto' and got past that thought,
My family moved into a neighborhood with the perception of a
better life,
Where both parents work together and men stayed married
to their wives,
However I came with a stigma on my head,
My parents were separated and I had a stepfather instead,
I didn't know the school that I was enrolled in had a rivalry going
with the school I'd transferred from,
When the students found out the school I transferred from they
made my days less than fun,

Now I was being bullied and didn't even
know what the word meant,
It was a 'target' on my back everywhere I went,
The children was envious cruel and very insensitive,
The hatred spread quickly even on the block I lived,
My mother wasn't aware she was always busy working,
She had no idea that I didn't fit in and that I was sad and hurting,
I learned some things while living in the 'county',
That everything that look good ain't really about it!

The Drunk...

The drunk, he dont drink, he drank;
And when he do he stank:
The smell of acholol coming out through his pores;
Makes you open all the windows, and the doors:
He needs to stop drinking, and start thinking;
Because, the dendrites in his brain, is shrinking:
The thoughts in his mind are all fuzz;
Cause, he chooses to walk around with a buzz:
They act as if they don't remember
what they did, when they were drunk;
But, a drunk is just a sober mind, that's stuck:
They can't filter out the things that they unconsciously longed;
When, drinking those thoughts they proudly own:
When sober they know how to distinctively pause;
But, drunk they're a rebel without a cause:
When drunk, they're causing all sorts of confusion;
Then sober they're left to deal with the conclusion:
Their behavior is inexcusable and affects all around;
And it's embarrassing to the ones that's close to them, when they
don't shut up or sit down:
Nevertheless, they still continue down the same destructive road;
Not only is a deteriorating their body
organs, is destroying their soul:
Some days are elusive, and others are not;
But they'll deny you an answer, by saying they simply forgot:

They avoid responsibilities and demands of all kind;
And, eventually lose touch with reality and acquire
a reprobate mind:
So, if you have a drunk, or know a drunk, stay clear of that spirit;
Because, whatever you stand for, they're not trying to hear it:
They can go into a rehabilitation center to get some help;
But, without a spiritual connection they're left by themselves:
The alcohol demons or in their heads and going to stay;
Unless they humble themselves and begin to pray;
They must pray for deliverance, and healing to come;
And God will fulfill it, that's why he sent his son:

Chapter 5

Entertainment

1. Magic-man...
2. Bite Dog ... Bite...
3. It's Just That...
4. The Cruise...
5. Bad Dog...Good Dog...
6. My 'Fans'...
7. Boogie Boogie Stump Jump...
8. The Goodnight Sleep...
9. A Knock at my Door...
10. What's Love...
11. The Twins...
12. Girls Trip...
13. Change the Station...

Magic-man...

I am a fraction more than my creation,
I have the power to satisfy every one of your sensations,
You're entitled to the best from me,
I'm equip to deliver with ecstasy,
I'm your 'Magic-man' with all the tricks of life in my hand,
Baby I hope you're able to understand,
That I'll fulfill your fantasies on demand,
Everyone I touch needs to appreciate,
Because the things I do are very great,
I'm able to grant you happiness,
No need to settle for nothing less,
I'm your 'Magic-man I'll do whatever it takes whenever I can,
That's my purpose that's my plan,
I'll take you further than you can imagine,
You'll be filled with wonders that you can't handle,
Now put your trust in my hand,
I'm your 'Magic-man!

Bite Dog...Bite....

The dog can't bite if he don't got teeth,
He won't bite if you got tough meat,

Dog won't bite in the day light,
Dog won't bite if he don't got no appetite,

Dog can't bite when it's time to fight,
If his teeth get knock out late at night,

Dog won't bite if he don't like the crowd,
Dog won't bite if the music too loud,

Dog can't bite if he's on the move,
Dog won't bite if your skin not smooth,

Dog can't bite at the end of the week,
If all he got left is old people to eat,

Dog won't bite if he's doing good,
Dog won't bite if he's misunderstood,

Dog won't bite in the sun light,
If he don't know his left from his right,

Dog won't bite if he lost his front teeth,
Dog won't bite if your meat not sweet,

Dog can't bite if his teeth get cracked,
Dog won't bite if he don't see black,

Dog won't bite if he's scary,
Dog won't bite if your skin too hairy,

Dog can't bite if he's not able,
Dog won't bite if he's at the wrong table,

Dog won't bite if you call him names,
Dog won't bite if he goes insane,

Dog won't bite if he went to sleep,
Dog won't bite if you got funky feet,

Dog won't bite if meat ain't fine,
Dog won't bite if he's drunk off wine,

Dog won't bite if it ain't nice and neat,
Dog won't bite no brunt up meat,

Dog won't bite if it's late in the evening,,
Dog can't bite if he ain't breathing,

Dog won't bite if he don't have a reason,
Dog won't bite if the meat out of season,

Dog won't bite if he's out in the rain,
Dog won't bite if he ain't got no brain,

Dog won't bite if his teeth ain't floss,
Dog can't bite if his teeth get loss,

Dog won't bite if he ain't got no bone,
Dog won't bite if his company gone home.

It's just that...

If it doesn't apply then let it fly,
If It don't fit you must forget,
If you're in a rush then make a fuss,
If you want to survive then stay alive,
If you don't use it you will lose it,
If it ain't right then take a hike,
If you want it right then stay the night,
If you want to tell then shout and yell,
If you want to scream then make a scene,
If in doubt then throw it out,
If it's large it's in charge,
If you can feel then it's real,
If you know it then show it,
If you live it then give it,
If you find it then keep it hid,
If you 'reap' it then keep it,
If it's a fact it's just that!

The Cruise...

On the other side of the world that's me,
Cruising on a ship in the middle of the sea,
On a big ship fighting through the ocean tide,
It's a lot of us cruising who wanted to ride,
We're sailing together through life mysteries,
But each of us aboard knows our destiny,
We're scheduled to stop on three tropical islands,
To admire their beauty and learn the culture inside of them,
All the souvenirs that I could possibly buy,
From the different cultures that I desire,
To taste their food will be a treat,
I heard that they have a crafty way to prepare their meet,
Their seafood is fresh and sure to get you full,
It's all-you-can-eat straight from the ocean's shore,
They speak of the desert that's rich and pure,
Made with the finest ingredients to keep you wanting more,
There are different restaurants on the upper level,
They serve a variety of cuisines that goes on forever,
There's lots of things that you can do on the boat,
There's a giant water slide and even a float,
There's live performances and indoor theatre as well,

Just for your entertainment to ensure your visit goes swell,
You all should come and join the fun,
Is going to be a memorable trip for everyone,
Oh, did you think I was already there,
No, I just heard all about it and decided to share.

Bad Dog...Good Dog...

Beneath the dark surface and roughness of a bark,
There's a gentle 'little' puppy cooing in the dark,
Just afraid of you as you are of-he,
Anxiously awaiting on what your next move shall be,
Now this dog is large and very vicious,
And he launches at you with bad intentions,
You take off running and he gave chase,
Only to knock you down and lick your face,
He throws his paws on your chest to pin you down,
Then slobs on your face and drools all around,
Now you think to yourself did he just kiss me,
And you look around for anyone else to see,
You tried to scream but couldn't get the words out,
And at that moment he licked you right in the mouth,
Then you jumped up and started throwing a 'fit',
You said that you would've been better off if you just got 'bit',
The owner of the dog finally came outside,
When he seen the two of you, he wasn't surprised,
Then he responded by saying "Oh I see you made another friend",
"Good dog good dog now come on in"!

My 'Fans'...

My 'fans', my 'fans', come clap your hands
They come to cheer for me, on demand:
Your loyalty is what got me here;
Of course I'll acknowledge you, when I'm near:
I've always gotten your full support;
And, I appreciate it, with all my heart:
For 'you' all my life revolves around;
So, please continue the cheerful sounds:
I need to hear your voices loud;
So, please scream and shout and give your applause:
It's okay to like me now;
Because, I mingle with the crowd:
For you are my fans, and I am yours,
Cause it's your applause, that I adore:
You mean as much to me, as I mean to you;
So, you need to know that I love you too:
You are my 'fans' and that's okay;
Cause, I'll be here for you, on any day:
I'll show up to see you day, or night;
And you'll cheer me on to make it right,
You all came out just to see;
And, that alone means the world to me:
You brought me joy, when you came to cheer and laugh;
And you did it all on my behalf:
I felt all love throughout the air;

You let me know you really care:
You need to know I love you more:
Because I never had any 'fans' before:

Boogie Boogie Stump Jump...

Boogie boogie jump,
Boogie boogie jump,
Kris Kross stump,
Kris Kross stump,
Stump jump lock,
Stump jump lock,
Then spin around and around and stop,,
Stutt down get up jump,
Stutt down get up jump,
Spin Kross Stump,
Spin Kross Stump,
Then spin around and around and stop,,
Boogie boogie jump
Kris Kross Stump,
Kris Kross Stump,
Stump jump lock,
Stump jump lock,
Then spin around and around and stop,
Stutt down get up jump,
Stutt down get up jump,
Spin Kross Stump,
Spin Kross Stump,
Then spin around and around and stop.

The Goodnight Sleep...

My friend came to town,
We both were excited we talked for a while,
She slept with me cause she's kind of spoiled,
I was very uncomfortable cause I'm sort of 'large',
She snored loudly all night in by ear,
Her 'snoring' and 'snorkeling' was the only thing I could hear,
While she snored all night I coughed and wheezed,
It was allergy season I couldn't help but sneeze,
I tried my best to keep her awake,
But she snored right through it for heaven's sake!
I'd dozed off for a few minutes,
I think that was the only sleep I was planning on getting,
Regardless I was glad that she came,
But her loud snoring nearly drove me insane,
All of a sudden it got quite was she awake?
I laid there wondering with no sound to make,
The night was over and my sleep finally came,
But then I heard her calling out my name,
She call out to me as she said "good morning",
And I 'grit' my teeth as I was yawning,
I hadn't slept a 'wink' but it's okay,
Cause just having her there brighten my day.

A knock at my door...

A stranger knocked on my door earlier o'clock,
Asking if someone was there and I answered no he's not
I said "who are you and what do you want"?
He said that he was his brother and he was pretty blunt,
I said "man no you're not".
Quit lying you need to stop,
Then he said "But I am his brother",
"Just from a different mother",
Then I said "get off my porch and I'm not going to fuss",
"I'm not trying to hear that 'ghetto- street" stuff",
as if he couldn't figure it out,
Looking real suspect with a gold 'grill' in his mouth,
I say he wasn't welcome but he refuse to take the hint,
I let my 'German Shepherd' out and he jumped off my porch cause
he didn't want to get 'bit'!

What's Love...

What is that romantic word with a gesture,
We all go after it with a question,
Find it in our hearts so smooth,
Breaking all of life's golden rules,
Overwhelming impulses beyond control,
With endless measures to bear our soul,
Hopelessly pondering for a conclusion,
Always trying to avoid its confusion,
Selfishly needing it all to ourselves,
Never willing to share with anyone else,
Desiring it to last on past forever,
If I could bottle it and preserve it that would be very clever,
Letting it define our very being,
Only to lose it between the scene,
Was it ever mine to hold or have,
Or was it just given on my behalf,
There's lots to loan that's no secret,
You can only borrow it you can't keep it,
Was it yours to give or did you just pretend,
Now that's not how to treat a friend,
I want more and more so I'll feel right,
I'm trying to grab hold with all my might,

SOARING

What makes this word so complicated?
When you get the answer please do relate it,
I referring to the feelings above,
Trying desperately to understand what's love!

The Twins...

The twins born identical five minutes apart,
Born together but not sharing the same heart,
Now their mother was flattered when the doctor brought them out,
Little did she know they'll have the same thought,
It was lucky for her she had two sides,
Because they both wanted to 'nurse' at the same time,
Together they ate and together they slept,
They laughed together and together they wept,
Now their mother would dress them just alike,
And no one could tell them apart day or night,
However she knew one from the other,
She had no problem she was their mother,
One of the twin was bad and the other one was good,
And they would play tricks on the kids in the neighborhood,
They would get into mischief and take off running,
When you gave chase they thought it was funny,
The teachers at school didn't know the difference,
One would sit in for the other when one was missing,
When they started to date they got a big laugh,
One of them would kiss you the first day then the next day you'll
kiss the other half,
Even their voices sound the same,
The only thing different was their names,
They looked just alike they talked alike and they danced alike,
They walked alike they sang alike and they dressed alike,

No one could tell them apart even in broad daylight,
Now they had some siblings who they 'worked' their nerves,
They would get into mischief and wouldn't say a word,
Now they were particularly fond of their older sister,
Because she would take them around everywhere with her,
When she wanted privacy she would duck and hide,
But they would shout her name loudly and begin to 'whine',
There was no escaping those cute little twins,
They were determine to annoy her until the day end,
Now they grew up and started their own lives,
Both of them had children and became a wife,
I am a daughter of one of the twins,
I didn't know which-was-which and that's where the fun began,
As-long-as I was at home with my own mother,
I didn't worry much about my aunt the other,
But when they got together it was hard as can be,
I couldn't tell one from the other with them
both looking right at me,
I remember calling "Mama Mama" one day in distress,
I was just a little person pulling at her dress,
But I didn't know it was my aunt until she started to speak,
She said "girl I ain't none of your mama and I told you the same
thing last week"!
I ran out the room feeling sad and confused,
And I cried even louder after I heard the news,
Then my mama comforted me to no surprise,
But I was tired of seeing doubles before my eyes,
But when I grew up I used it to my advantage,
When I was suspended from school my aunt reinstated me so my
mother didn't panic,
The teachers at my school they never knew the difference,
They were giving my aunt the lecture as if she was listening,
Ok so you get it my aunt was the rowdy of the two,
She never really followed any rules and always did what she
wanted to do,
When they were young adults my mama was a calm home-body,
On-the-other-hand my aunt was loud and always wanted to party,

But when they got older their roles switched,
And everyone was able to tell which one was which,
My mother became anxious obnoxious and always on the go,
Whereas my aunt became calm mild and didn't want to
party no more,
My mother shared with me a story about their childhood,
They use to play this game called 'think fast' and throw something
and the other one will catch it if they could,
My mother threw a porcelain doll and my aunt missed
It knocked out her front tooth leaving a gap when she
smiled or kissed,
Then 30 years later almost to the precise day,
My mother dived in shallow water and knocked out the exact same
tooth in a different way,
Who knew the twins would follow the other,
I'm just glad to this day I know which ones my mother,
They still dress alike every chance they get,
Cause they're an identical twins and they don't want
the world to forget!

Girls Trip...?

On the road we're about to go,
Four hours later none of us would know,
All the fun and laughter we had in store,
Make it last forever cause we needed more,
All of us where from different walks of life,
One of them I've known my entire life,
One of them I've known for about half the way,
And the last one I just meet the other day,
So we rented a car and tried to packed it for the road,
To take a girl's trip before we got to old,
But one of us packed 'way' too much,
So I drove my truck instead to avoid the fuss,
I cooked lots of food and brought snacks also,
We stuffed our luggage in and we were ready to roll,
There was a special event that we were scheduled to see,
And the rest of the itinerary was planned by me.

Change the 'station'...

Man change the station and do it quick
I don't wanna listen to that man tricks,
I don't want to hear a bunch 'A.D.D.' rapper throwing a fit,
I'm not sixteen I don't want to hear them trying to be slick,
They singing their "game' is lame,
And can't even spell their names,
He supposed to be an old 'G',
But trying to rap to a young sweetie,
Dude you need to step down cause you washed up,
You ain't bout that life so shut up!
He talking about break it down,
But he need to get somewhere and sit 'it' down,
He said "bag it up working hard trying to get it",
But he ain't nothing and he ain't with it,
So he need to just forget about it,
This trash 'slain' you listen to,
Cause you ain't got nothing better to do,
Change the station this ain't my style,
I don't wanna hear a grown 'man-child",
Some people never grow up they just get older,
And they don't mature they actually get slower,
This man is past forty,
Rapping 'turn-up' where's the party,
This man he's somebody grandfather,
Still chasing skirts trying to holla,

SOARING

The girls he want are barely legal,
And few months younger he'd gotten the 'needle',
That's why I can't listen to this trash,
So change the station and get some 'class'!

Chapter 6

Special Dedication

1. My Friend...
2. Magical Love...
3. Mister...

My Friend...

All of the qualities of a true friend you possess,
As a friend of mine you're one of the best,
Under any circumstances we could've met,
And we still would've been friends I bet,
Your spirit radiates a pleasant a glow,
It's sure to bring about smiles wherever you go,
I don't know much about you-you know,
However I'm pleased with the things that you show,
You don't have to be with someone every day to be their friend,
You just need to appreciate the kindness
that they're willing to lend,
I'm glad to have met your acquaintance,
When I see you your presence makes my day a little brighter,
Thank you for all the kindness you've shown,
As a friend I happy to say you're my own,
I hope that I made you 'blush' with this simple poem,
Because my intentions were to turn on my charm.

Dedicated to "Harry"

Magical Love...

That magical love stuck in time,
Priceless moments were yours and mine,
With all of your compassion you stole my heart,
Without hesitation you did your part,
You educated me on so many different levels,
Because that's what kind of guy you were 'pretty-cool' yet clever,
I loved the way you moved on the dance floor,
Dressed so 'sharp' as you put on a show,
Dazzling all the ladies there with your charm,
But I was the only girl you chose to be on your arms,
I had to get use to your stubborn ways,
When I did we complimented each other days,

I was impressed by the way you handle my personality,
You knew the right touch to give me a 'dose of reality'!
The adventures we shared were one of a kind,
Making precious memories to last a life time,
You were strong until the end nevertheless
when you called it made me cry
,
You tried to prepare me for the day we all will say goodbye,
My plans were to love you through the upcoming years,
But you 'left' me and I'm heartbroken filled with endless tears,

SOARING

You were my life and our love I'll miss,
I'll mourn today as I seal it with a kiss!

In loving Memories: William Tomlin
                          (8-26-1949)-(10-16-2017)
         With Love: Simone Knox

Mister...

My first mister strong and brave,
Yet gentle and concern,
The respect I have for him over the years he earned,
He came into my life when I was at the age of three,
He was kind enough to be a father to me,
He taught me a lot over the years,
How to show courage and overcome my fears,
He taught me to fish hunt and spot a deer on sight,
In 'spite' of being a 'female' I turned out just right,
Awe I'm just (joking) it was a big delight,
He didn't have any sons so I was up for the 'fight',
I did some things that were contrary to being a lady,
I was a true 'tomboy' and I acted pretty shady,
I hung out in pool-halls with my cap turn to the back,
Wearing blue jeans and high-top tennis shoes
and I even shot 'craps',
I was hard as they come and had no fear,
If you got into a match with me you'll shed the first tear,
Yes he had me together 'all right' and in 'them'
streets standing 'tall',
I was well-rounded and educated above all,
He taught me how to count my money and spell at the age of three,
I was reading for all his friends and they would pay me,
He taught me how to hustle and survive in 'them' streets,
He taught me how to be a lady on Sundays

and stay humble and sweet,
He taught me Christian values and he kept us in church,
He supported our family cause he hustled and worked,
I got hit by a car and was confined to a bed for a while,
Doing that time he took care of me showing his gentle style,
He nursed me back to health and taught me to walk all over again,
He taught me to show humility and
how to become my own best friend,
Then he went out and bought a new car it was my 'backseat' and
there wasn't any room left,
I didn't want my siblings around me I just wanted to be by myself,
When we went on family outings my siblings road
with my mother,
I road in my 'backseat' and we trailed each other,
I was his 'princess' spoiled as could be,
He was my 'hero' who was there to you protect me,
He loved me a lot and everyone around thought he was my 'dad',
He called me his 'daughter' which made my heart glad,
I loved him to the moon and the stars-shine bright,
He was always there to tuck me in at night,
With him it was love and kindness all the way,
He raised me with respect and value for my day,
When I had my first daughter he cared for her as well,
But he was disappointed I wasn't married in his heart-I could tell,
Sickness came over his body and God called him home young,
And at that moment I felt so alone,
There'll always be love and sadness when I think of his name,
But all the precious memories we shared will always remain!

In loving memories of: Henry White
                                          Aka "Fat"